Chinese Traditions: From Festivals to Funerals

May-Blossom Chang Wilkinson

Chinese Traditions: From Festivals to Funerals
Published 2020
Printed in the United States of America
ISBN: 978-0-9970123-2-3

Library of Congress Cataloging-in-Publication Data

Editor/Publisher: Willy Chang Wilkinson
Hapa Papa Press
PO Box 27401
Oakland, CA 94602
www.willywilkinson.com

HPP
Hapa Papa Press

Dedication

This collection of stories is dedicated to my mother, Gam Pung, who told them to me, her only daughter, while in the kitchen, laundry room, or while occupied with other household tasks, previously passed down to her by a long chain of storytellers and tradition keepers.

Table of Contents

The Annual Chinese (Lunar) Calendar

Early one morning the Ox woke with a premonition that action was required of him. He had dreamt that the Buddha was not long for this world. "I must go and see him, and tell him how much we value his teachings, especially how he wants the world to profit from his words."

He quickly prepared himself and started out to see the Buddha. On the way he passed a Tiger, who asked, "Where are you going so early in the morning and in such a hurry?" The Ox replied, "I have heard Buddha is not long for this world. I want to see him and thank him personally for his teachings, for us to appreciate and preserve the Environment for all to enjoy."

"Oh, wait for me," said the Tiger. "I want to tell him how happy he has made me by telling people to love and value the lives of all animals, with feet or without." And he trudged off behind the Ox. As they walked on they passed a

Rabbit, who asked, "Where are you two going in such a hurry? They repeated the message that the Buddha was not long for this world and they wanted to see him and receive his blessing to continue living effectively in this world.

"Oh, wait for me. I want to go with you. I want to thank him for making me aware of weather conditions to help us prepare our homes and family for rain, fine weather, heat, cold and wind." And he joined the Ox and the Tiger. As they trudged along, they passed a Dragon who asked the same question.

Upon their reply, the Dragon said, "I will join you. I want to thank the Great Buddha for making us aware of the five blessings that we should all aspire to: Long life, Riches, Tranquility, a Love of Virtue, and a Happy Ending."

They passed a Serpent wriggling midst rocks, a Horse, a Ram, a Mouse, who all wanted to join the procession, each with a specific purpose, to thank the Buddha for alerting them to the Five Elements (water, fire, wood, metal, and earth) and the Five Tastes (salty, bitter, sour, sweet, and fiery).

The Monkey and Rooster joined them with the wish to thank the Buddha for the knowledge of the Five Poisons (the kiss of a Centipede, Scorpion, Spider, Toad and Viper).

The Horse wanted to thank the Buddha for alerting the world to the four supernatural creatures that presided over the four sides of the universe and the four seasons: Dragon (East, Spring), the Divine Tortoise (North, Winter), the Phoenix (South, Summer), and the White Tiger (West, Autumn).

The Dog and the Boar rushed to keep up with the parade of devoted animals and indicated their wish to thank Buddha for the Four Treasures, each with a double purpose: for INK, which had a double purpose for transcription, and a cure for convulsions; PAPER, which, when burned, could be used as a charm against infectious diseases; the BRUSH PEN, made of sable, fox or rabbit hairs set in a bamboo holder; and the INK SLAB, made of stone and paste, used to prepare the ink for writing.

This motley crew reached a body of water, a stream with very clear water on the surface. They could see that on the other side was a pallet with a figure reclining on it, underneath trees and by some flowers blooming on the ground.

"There is the Buddha resting and looking so calm and serene. Let us all swim across to thank him and receive his blessing!!!" As they prepared to swim across, the little Mouse jumped up and down and with great concern, squeaked, "I will not be able to swim the distance. I will surely drown!" The kindly Ox said, "You'll be all right. Just jump on my head and I will take you across, dry."

As they reached the other side, the animals took time to shake themselves dry before approaching the Buddha. The mouse, who was the only animal not wet, leaped from the Ox's head and quickly ran to the Buddha, while the others followed. As the Ox said, "I was the first to come to you," the Mouse said "No, I was!!!" And Buddha replied, "Yes, Mouse came to me first. I will give you twelve animals the honor of a year on the Lunar Calendar.

This explains the existence of the Lunar Calendar with its twelve-year cycle of animals, with the Mouse at the beginning, and each succeeding year honoring, after the Mouse, the Ox (or sometime called Cow), Tiger, Hare (Rabbit), Dragon, Serpent (Snake), Horse, Ram or (Goat), Monkey, Rooster, Dog and Boar (or wild mountain Pig).

The lunar calendar is plotted by divination. The beginning of the New Year starts on the first New Moon after the Winter Solstice. Seven years out of nineteen an extra month is added to make up for the days lost during those years.

Rewritten Winter 2014

Celebration of the Chinese New Year

The first day of the Chinese Lunar Calendar was a very important event in our family. In the month leading up to it only good words are said, new clothes are prepared to wear on that day, all debts are paid, and hair is groomed (washed or cut) before that day. Ten days before, the paper picture of the Kitchen God, which has been mounted in the kitchen over the stove this past year, is taken down, his lips rubbed with honey, and ceremonially burned in a temple blessed container, thereby sending him on his way to report to the heavenly gods and goddesses on the good and bad (if any) activities of this family during the past year. The honey on his lips is to ensure that only pleasant activities in this household are reported.

On the morning of that day, I remember my mother rising at about 4:30 AM to prepare the vegetarian breakfast. Later, the children would rise, dressed in their new clothes. The bedroom in order, we would approach in order of birth, our parents who were now seated in the living room in their new clothes, and pour tea, passing out candied fruits and vegetables from the eight-segmented Tray of Togetherness to add to the tea and to receive the blessings for the new year. The oldest child does this first, then sits down, followed by the next oldest, who pours to the parents and to the oldest child already seated. More goodies from the Tray of Togetherness are added to the tea cups.

By the time it was my turn, I, being the youngest, was faced with my parents' and older siblings' teacups piled high with candied sweets and a wee bit of tea. Then, my father rose and served ME – to the great surprise of my brothers – and we all added ginger to the tea, a must for strength. There was also a special sticky rice pudding steamed especially for the New Year—sticky to imply family cohesiveness—as well as ceremonial foods to be eaten on that day.

Before leaving the room, each of us stepped forward and performed the act of obeisance—on one knee, head bowed respectfully, with folded hands—as we received the annual blessings and "red paper money" to be spent on something sweet during the next fifteen days. (The envelope is not to be opened until later and not in the presence of the donor.)

The blessing includes three important aspects of a peaceful and productive life:
"Remember your ancestors,
Honor your parents, and
Always RESPECT your teachers because they prepare you for the better life."

Each year I have taught this to my students. My mother believed that this blessing should be said all year. One parent wondered if I was "brainwashing" my students.

For those who used jai for religious purposes, it is strictly vegetarian with no meat or meat flavoring. However, for general consumption of "cheong jai," one could add chicken broth, oyster sauce, or dried oysters to enrich the flavor. In addition, one can use gelatin, and the black Nori Maki, a seafood covering used in Sushi. On the beaches I have found live sea urchins, to be eaten raw, also to be found in first class Japanese restaurants. I added broccoli, green peas, bottled raw oysters, carrots, tulip bulbs, wood and cloud fungus, and hydrated oysters to my "vegetarian dish." I was able to find two spots on the Pacific Coast, 2400 miles from Hawaii, where I harvested seaweed and seaweed families like that I had grown up with in Hawaii.

As the day grew near, for the "made" or purchased item for the house, I crocheted some anti-macassars for the living room chairs, since I had learned the art as one of the "new things" one year as my "learn something new" project.

For fifteen days the celebration is with family and close relatives. That is why parades are always held two weeks after the first day of the New Year.

Chinese Table Etiquette

A common Chinese greeting is "Have you eaten yet?"

It is an inquiry into the state of one's well-being and condition. The polite response is "Yes!" even if you haven't eaten in the past twelve hours and are feeling hypoglycemic. The greeting is extended in kindness only and not meant as a literal inquiry. This greeting arises from when food was not always plentiful (in China) and well-being was equated with having eaten a meal. Dining in a traditional setting with the Chinese does not require an etiquette lesson. However, being familiar with a few cultural nuances will build confidence and provide an opportunity to impress your companions, whether at a grand banquet ballroom or the home of a Chinese friend.

In fact, on December 11, 1941, four days after the Japanese bombed Pearl Harbor to begin World War II, that was the question my father asked my fourth brother, who was away at Medical School in Omaha, Nebraska. He had no way of knowing whether we were dead or alive, since he heard that bombs had been dropped near our restaurant in Wahiawa, near heavily-bombed Schofield Barracks. We had been put on the waiting list for out-going phone calls to the 'mainland. All Fourth Brother could say in response to Papa's polite question was:

"Are YOU all right? Is everyone all right?"

Gift-giving is a customary formality and an expression of appreciation for a dining invitation. The Chinese are generous and will rarely enter a friend's home—especially for the first time—empty-handed. It's a sign of respect, acceptance of friendship, and thanks for the privilege of being invited. Gift-giving is a way to maintain "face." It allows the guest to reciprocate the invitation with an advance token. The hostess will usually remark that a gift was not necessary and that the guest shouldn't have gone to the trouble for just a "small, simple" meal. But when the comment is translated into Chinese, it's a compliment, because the action of your generosity and effort will leave a lasting impression.

The appropriate gift item often depends on your relationship to the Chinese host, hostess and family. When visiting a relative's home, food items are appropriate, such as fresh seasonal fruit (oranges, apples, Asian pears, persimmons), candy, cookies, Chinese preserved fruit, and cured beef jerky. If visiting during the day, dim sum, pastries, and buns are also appropriate. Chinese elders would especially appreciate luxury items such as dried black mushrooms, dried scallops, shark's fin, bird's nest, Chinese sausage, canned abalone, tea, a bottle of rice wine, or even "mao tai." When compiling the gift package, select an odd, or yang, number of items, as it relates to the living. Eight is also a good number because it connotes prosperity. Never give four items; the number four is bad luck, because it sounds like the word for death.

Gifts for business and social acquaintances are more formal. Appropriate items could reflect the hosting family's interests and hobbies, such as sports memorabilia, illustrated or pictorial coffee table books, decorative items for the home, a bottle of fine whisky or cognac, gourmet chocolates, or other luxury items. If the hosts have children, popular choices are toys, games, and play clothes with contemporary cartoon characters.

Always present wrapped gifts to your host. Consider wrapping in colors fortuitous to the Chinese: red, gold, yellow, or pink. Avoid wrapping in white or black, as they are associated with funerals. Also reconsider green (the color of separation) and blue (the color of mourning).

Never give a clock because the Chinese associate it with death. The word for clock, "jung," sounds like the Cantonese word for funeral. Watches, on the other hand, are popular and contemporary accessories, as well as being functional. Knives and scissors are inappropriate gifts, especially for business associates, as these items represent severing ties. The Taiwanese do not give umbrellas because the word for umbrella sounds like the word for separation. Handkerchiefs and white flowers are off-limits because they are also associated with funerals. Nowadays, cut flowers are becoming more acceptable as a business gift because of relaxed belief with the old superstitions. But little old ladies would still cringe at the sight of them. When in doubt, give a living potted plant.

Always present and accept a gift with two hands as a sign of respect, reverence, and sincerity.

It is not customary for the Chinese to open gifts in front of the giver. They will generously accept the gift and put it aside for opening after the guests have departed. The purpose of this custom is twofold: first, the Chinese consider impatience and selfishness taboo. Second, it spares embarrassment to the giver and receiver should the gift not be pleasing, thus "saving face" for all involved. Moreover, the Chinese typically do not send thank-you notes, although many have adopted this gesture in America, depending on the situation in which a gift was bestowed. Because the gratitude has been expressed in person at the time of accepting the gift, the Chinese feel a written formality is redundant.

An invitation to dine in a Chinese home is a great honor. It's the ultimate compliment to a friendship, as many Chinese are culturally reserved about the intimacy and privacy of their homes and instead prefer to entertain in a restaurant. This custom arises from the days when the typical home was too small to accommodate any but the family's residents.

Upon entering a Chinese home, if you spot a shoe collection at the entryway, you should also remove your shoes. Follow your Chinese host's lead as to where to sit for the evening. Don't wander through the house even when offered a tour of the house. When touring, always follow, and always allow the older members to enter a room out of respect.

When dinner is served, again, take your host's lead for when to begin drinking and eating. Often, a toast of friendship and appreciation for the evening will be given at the meal's start. When dining in a home, respectfully serving the elders first still applies—as does serving the guest seated next to you—until they politely excuse you from the gesture. In any case, serving yourself should always come last.

For a pleasant dining experience, keep dinner conversation to light social topics. Save world politics, the state of the nation, or the evolving economy for another time. Conversation should gravitate to the meal's tastiness and the host's efforts in preparing the dishes. At the meal's end, it's acceptable to the Chinese to use a toothpick discreetly at the table by moving the pick with one hand while covering the entire mouth with the other. When it's time to clear the table, it's polite to offer to help but highly unlikely you'll be taken up on it.

Favorite Indoor Sport of The Chinese

Many columnists writing about China have indicated that "the favorite indoor sport of the Chinese people is COOKING." Then there are others who follow that comment with, "The next favorite indoor sport is EATING what has been prepared." Keen observers continue to say that another invaluable sport, if we may call it a "sport," is the fellowship and sharing of thoughts and ideas that occur among people sharing a meal together. It is the most unique gift of all.

The conversation that occurs around a table laden with dishes of specially prepared food in small serving sizes often brings out ideas and thoughts as the diners eat and enjoy each other's comments, whether it is about current news, children's accomplishments, or personal hopes and family goals.

Because now people gather around a table laden with food in small sizes for lunch as they convey ideas or present proposals for business decrees. This is how "Dim Sum" developed. The literal translation is "dot heart." Poetically, it means "heart's delight." An appropriate explanation for dim sum is that they are delicious, tiny, little bite-size morsels of stuffed savory meat or sweet dumplings--either deep-fried, baked or steamed, and served with a variety of tasty, hot, or spicy dips.

These are brought out by waiters or waitresses on small plates and, as the waiter calls out the name of the dish, a hungry person may take what is chosen. At the end of the meal the waiter counts the number of plates left (now empty) and relates the cost of the entire meal.

One day, a special event caused my father to close our restaurant and travel to downtown Honolulu to a "dim sum" restaurant just opened by a close family friend. Our whole family attended—my parents, my four brothers, and ME—SEVEN of us.

When it came time for us to leave, the waitress counted the number of plates and told us the cost of the luncheon. She then remarked, "For the seven of you, this is an unusually low price." My father agreed with her and said, "Yes, you're right. But you see the empty plates," and he paid her what she requested.

Outside the restaurant and on our way to the car, Second Brother pulled out a plate from his front pants pocket and handed it to my father. He continued to pull out a plate from his various pockets—six in all!

"You were cheating our friend!" and he gathered up the six plates and returned to the restaurant and explained to the owner (his friend of long standing), what my brother had done and how he and the waitress had both wondered how seven people could have eaten so little. It was a lesson for us of honesty and trust.

It took a while for these "dim sum" restaurants to take hold. At first, they were meant for businessmen to conduct their work, so the restaurants sold "dim sum" from ten AM to two PM.

In 1960 when I arrived in San Francisco on my way to a conference as a representative of the Hawaiian Congregational Christian Churches, two of my brothers happened to be in San Francisco on their way home to Honolulu. They wanted to take me out to lunch in Chinatown. At that time, there were only two restaurants that had dim sum on their menu.

We were refused entrance when I appeared. They said they did not serve women between ten and two because those were the hours men were conducting business with their clients. After some pleading, we were allowed in to a small tea table far back, next to the kitchen door. They seated me with my back to the front of the restaurant, so that I would not be visible to the other patrons dining and doing business there.

Instead of just two restaurants serving all of Chinatown, now there are about ten such restaurants on each block.

A Scholar's Invention

Once upon a time, a very, very long time ago, it was the custom of the Emperor of China to invite scholars to live with him in his palace for a short time, on a rotating basis, so that he could become acquainted with the men who had created and developed so many inventions which have subsequently become useful not only to the Chinese people but to people from other countries in the "outside world."

China is known for developing the process of making silk, a paper-making process, block printing, porcelain, the magnetic compass, gunpowder for fireworks, and an earthquake-detecting device, to name a few.

To qualify and keep the title of Scholar, some distinctive writing, research, artwork, or useful invention had to be created for public scrutiny and subsequent use.

Those invited to dine at the Emperor's Table were seated according to rank and value of inventions. Bowls of prepared food were brought to the center of a large rectangular table, in front of the Emperor, who sat in the center. The most favored Scholars were seated next to him or across from him, close to the bowls of food. Those yet to distinguish themselves were seated at both ends.

In the center of each bowl of food was a large serving spoon. At the place of each guest was a small bowl, a small plate, and a bowl with water for hand-washing. The only utensil was a spoon, and a towel for drying the hands after each washing.

Each participant would use the large serving spoons to serve themselves, then eat either with the spoon or by picking up food with their fingers...hence the finger bowl to cleanse their hands after handling the food. Those seated at both ends of the table had a difficult time reaching and serving themselves. There were times when they could not reach some of the bowls, so they went without.

One day, as the Emperor conversed and asked questions of his guests, he addressed one of the scholars at the end of the table: "Chang Mun-Gett! You have not come up with an invention for some time. It is time that you enrich our lives with something new, or you will not be invited to live here any longer. I want to hear of something creative soon, or Out You Go!!!"

That afternoon a very worried Chang Mun-Gett paced back and forth in the patio trying to come up with an invention. As he walked, deep in thought, suddenly he bumped his head against a branch of a tall tree. He thought to himself, *How silly of me. I did not see that tree branch.* He began pacing again, in another direction, but somehow bumped into the same tree branch again. When this happened a third time, in anger he swung at the tree branch, momentarily blaming his stupidity for running into the tree, and wondering why the branch was following him. As his hand hit the branch, the branch broke off the tree and little twigs fell from the branch to his feet.

He was saddened that he had hurt the tree, but, as he looked down at the dislodged twigs, he saw with surprise a pattern of sticks on the ground. He picked up a few and they immediately formed a continuation of his fingers. He walked around, picking up objects with the sticks. He thought, I'll be able to use these extensions to reach the food in the center bowl. And my hands will not get messy. I won't have to continually use the finger bowl to wash my hands, he thought. With the tool he always kept in his pocket, he smoothed out a pair of sticks, then decided to make another pair, and put them in his chest pocket.

That evening, at dinner, he calmly reached the foods so far away from him in the center of the table, did not say a word, did not have to use the finger bowl. In making conversation, the Emperor demanded, "Chang Mun-Gett. Do you have something new to report to me? Any inventions? Any new ideas?"

Chang Mun-Gett did not respond. He kept right on reaching for the food with his elongated fingers, put the food directly in his mouth, and did not have to use the finger bowl.

Suddenly, the Emperor said, "Chang Mun-Gett. What is that on your fingers? How can you eat without soiling your fingers?"

Chang Mun-Gett did not respond but went right on eating. In exasperation, the Emperor stood up and walked to the end of the table (which he never ever did) and demanded, "What do you have there? Let me see what is in your hand!"

With that, my ancestor stood up and demonstrated his new invention, and said, "Look! I have made an extra pair for you to use," handing him the extra pair he had stashed in his chest pocket.

The Emperor blessed him and said, "We must thank the Gods for sending this knowledge to you. These chopsticks shall always be used for cooking or eating, and not banged about uselessly, lest we offend the Gods who have given you this knowledge to share with the world."

That is the story I heard from my mother, who heard it from my father, who is descended from a long line of scholars.

Updated 13 March 2013

The Annual Kite Flying Festival

Every year, about two weeks after the Moon Festival
(observed on the fifteenth day of the eighth month of the lunar calendar) Papa
would arrive home from a busy day shopping downtown with several large
bundles under his arms.

"It's almost Kite Festival Day!" he would announce. Mama would quickly
check the Chinese Lunar Calendar on the wall and always respond:

"You're right! The ninth day of the ninth month will soon be here." And I
was instructed to go outside and fetch my brothers. This day usually occurred
late in September or early October on the Gregorian Calendar.

I watched with curious interest as father pulled each item from the bags: a
bundle of thin bamboo strips pre-cut to different lengths, a swatch of silk, a
rolled-up bundle of fine rice paper embedded with pressed rice and husks, and
several balls of very strong twine.

Meanwhile, Mama came out of the kitchen with a bowl of cold rice, a splash of water, and a spoon with a flattened round base and handed it to me, saying quietly:

"Mash these well; there can be no lumps." And so I did as I was told, preparing glue.

Papa soaked some bamboo strips of different lengths in the pan of water that Mama brought. Nature must have intended bamboo for making kite frames; it was modular, and each module is structured like a bird's bone. It is probably stronger than steel weight for weight, and it can be easily worked. After soaking, it can be split and bent into circles without much trouble, hence that exclusively Chinese kite, the caterpillar, with its several circular segments and leg-like stabilizers.

Papa and my brothers made several kites that day, preparing for the community observance next weekend. Holes were drilled in the ends as needed for noise making to enhance the music of the kite. Although this was strictly a male sport, Papa always made a small kite for me.

At the festival the following weekend it was fun to see the various creations. Some were shaped like spectacles or coins, and likenesses of lizards, butterflies, hawks. Those that made hawks attached steamers in such a way that the hawks could swoop and dive. One family grouped several bird kites tethered to a single cable and worked them like marionettes. There were hexagonal and octagonal kites without tails, and they swirled and tumbled so they flew like giant yo-yos.

It is recorded that kites first made their appearance in China in about the fourth Century BC. Silk was used first; father showed us the silk that he remembered his father using when he was a young child. When paper was invented in 300 BC it became the medium of choice because it was less expensive and more readily available. During kite flying time, which lasts several months, everyone who possibly can ascends to a high place—a hill or temple tower to escape a terrible calamity as predicted by an ancient sage. The warning is long forgotten, but the belief that "flying high" promotes longevity is preserved.

At first, kites were used as banners, or as scarecrows, observation posts, or divining instruments. From the tenth Century they were flown for fun. Kites did not reach Europe until the eighteenth Century, although Marco Polo reported seeing them during his travels to the Middle Kingdom.

At the Kite Festival, prizes were given for the one flying the highest, longest, the most colorful, or the most useful. Then came the second part of the festival—the killer part; each family was allowed to fly one kite, prepared for combat. To prepare a kite for this part of the festival, the last part of the string is soaked in starch or glue and dusted with powdered glass; this makes the string or cord both stiff and extremely sharp.

Two fliers will each try to sever the other's string by crossing over it and giving it a sharp snap. After "killing" one, the winner continues attacking others until only one remains: the WINNER. Then following the celebration; everyone is friendly again and a joyous feast is enjoyed by everyone with good words and singing.

In 2003 a young man born in Kabul, Afghanistan, Khaled Hosseini, wrote a book describing a similar activity in his native land. *The Kite Runner* was on the bestseller list for many years and the film was nominated for two Golden Globes and an Academy Award in 2007.

Did this festival come from China, or did someone from Kabul travel to China with this sport? It is interesting to note that nothing can be kept as the property of one country. Sports, crafts, and household conveniences all develop on their own as the need arises and creative geniuses from all cultures devise implements to meet those needs. The Kite Festival is an example of a custom not limited to one culture.

January 2009

Festival of The Hungry Ghosts

Throughout the year, at festival times, offerings are provided by local families for their departed members in the way of food, clothing, and other needs. Those departed souls without living family members have no one to provide for them in the way of food, clothing, and other objects that are important for a continuous comfortable life. Being so deprived, they are without daily necessities and so are dependent on good-hearted souls for their immediate necessary belongings, such as food, clothing, and home, to enable them to have a comfortable, productive life experience.

At a certain time each year, good-hearted, thoughtful souls see fit to provide for what they refer to as "hungry ghosts." At designated locations, food, clothing, and other objects are set out for them to enable a continuous comfortable life. This has been a continuous activity for generations and has become a part of a living tradition for the general populace with a day set aside for this activity—the fifteenth day of the seventh month on the lunar calendar.

In San Francisco, on several building walls in the Chinatown area, niches have been carved out with a flat ledge to hold incense, food, clothing, and other objects considered necessities for the "hungry ghosts." This activity, on the fifteenth day of the seventh month of the lunar calendar, considered traditional by Chinatown residents and "hungry ghosts," is a time looked forward to by local Chinatown residents and, of course, those without immediate family to provide for them.

Unfortunately, with the increase of homeless individuals in the 1980's in San Francisco, hungry people from areas not linked to San Francisco Chinatown, without the knowledge and understanding of this "sacred" activity, abused and caused damage to the ledges and objects on them. This caused many Chinatown residents to stop this practice, which had been a revered custom for generations. This change caused many "ghosts" to continue to be "hungry," and the gates of the underworld to remain "closed."

In my family, Mama designated many special "Hungry Ghost" days. There were evenings when I was to set another place at the dinner table. On "Cemetery Mornings" an area was arranged to indicate an invitation to a "hungry ghost" just in case there was someone close by in need of sustenance. This we did not only on the fifteenth day of the seventh month, but on other days when we felt the need.

And I always continued the day feeling much better for having fed a "hungry ghost."

11 September 2013

The Dragon Boat Festival

My widowed Grandma, whom we addressed as "PoPo," wanted her offspring (daughters, sons and grandchildren) to always remember the Chinese celebrations that occurred throughout the year, often observed at gatherings involving traditional food and legendary stories.

It seems that occasions arose every several weeks throughout the year for us to gather to once again hear the explanation of terrestrial events and to dine on the foods that occur to justify each planetary phenomenon.

I looked forward to these gatherings, not only for the food and stories, but also for the chance to play with my cousins. PoPo's large house was in the center of a large lot between two smaller units. There was a long, paved walk down the center to her home, which was set back from the street. Upon our arrival, we hurried down this walkway, up fifteen steps to the front porch, through the living room and into the dining area where PoPo sat in her wheelchair waiting for us.

We were taught to greet her first, go down on one knee with our hands clasped on the other knee, and say her name and indicate our happiness at seeing her and hope that all is well with her. I only remember her in a wheelchair, to which she was confined the last seven years of her life.

At each gathering, ceremonial foods were prepared to accompany the usual "basics." I especially enjoyed the feast observed on the fifth day of the fifth month on the lunar calendar, casually referred to as the Dragon Boat Festival.

History tells the legend of Chu Yuan, an honest Minister of the State of Chu, who lived in the feudal period of the Fourth Century B.C. Accused of wrong-doing and on the verge of suicide for political reasons, he wrote a poem about the worldly joys of food. He then later committed suicide by drowning, and his death came to be commemorated as the focus of the Dragon Boat Festival.

As the story goes, many centuries ago there was a period of continued violent torrential rains and storms that ruined many rice paddies and vegetable gardens. In prayers at the Chinese temples, the suffering, deprived farmers were told by the priests that the gods were angry because of the continued bickering among the farmers and their refusal to share and help those less fortunate. The continuing storms were a message from the River Dragons indicating their unhappiness because of the turmoil among the earth people.

The people threw food into the rivers for the River Dragons. Still the storms continued. Back to the temples for more advice. They were told that the food thrown by them were dispersed every which way when they hit the water and the River Dragons were not able to partake of them.

What to do? A vision appeared to the head farmer, telling him that food thrown unwrapped, could not reach the River Gods who dwelt on the lower section of the river bed. He was told to gather leaves of the bamboo plant, lotus and ti (spelled t-i, not t-e-a) and wrap food (rice, beans, egg yolks, sausage) in it, each package wrapped to show several triangles, tied with un-knotted string. This way the food could be picked up in one hand, the string opening the package with one pull, since the River Gods would not have on hand a knife to cut the string.

After listening to stories, we proceeded to the other side of the room and bowed three times at the altar, place three lighted incense sticks before the shrine of the Goddess Kwan Yin, and then retreated back to the front porch to show obeisance to the Earth God on the ground at the front door with three more sandalwood incense sticks.

This ritual was observed by each family as they arrived. The younger members gathered in the large lanai (porch) that surrounded half of the house while the older members retreated to the kitchen to prepare the food for the celebration. Since I was in the lower third, age-wise, of the thirty-one first cousins, I got to play until it was time to partake of the food containing the desired five points of direction—east, west, north, south and center. It was tied with strings of five colors (red, yellow, blue, black, white), which were the colors used on the original flag of China, tied and knotted in such a way that just one pull of the cord is needed to make the cooked food available to the River Dragons. They were able to partake of the food, and the storms subsided. This particular bundle of delicious concoction is lovingly called: JOONG. It is so popular, it is now available all year round in Chinese markets, not just on the fifth day of the fifth month, and is complete as a one-dish meal.

To enlarge on this festival, now, in all parts of the world, Dragon Boat races are held. Boats are decorated with a dragon's head on one end, and the tail on the other. Foster City holds one of the races on the fifth day of the fifth month on the lunar calendar, which usually occurs around the end of May and into June on the Gregorian calendar.

This year, 2011, the fifth day of the fifth month on the Lunar Calendar falls on June 6 on the Gregorian calendar. Locally there are Dragon Boat races wherever there is enough water. Boats are colorfully decorated as dragons, with two rows of people manning oars, facing a Coxswain chanting the rhythmic stroke for each oar, and indicating turns when necessary, to prevent collisions with other Dragon Boats in the San Francisco Bay.

Dragon Boat races are scheduled for the next several weekends, with a subsequent feasting after each event. There will be ti-leaf triangular wrapped Joong, with various fillings, to be enjoyed by the participants, after each race.

The goal is not the feast. It is the memory of famous scholar-statesman Chu Yuan being honored that is the primary reason for this observance.

1 June 2011.

Legend of The Chang Family

It is recorded that the first known Chang, written and
pronounced Jang (in Cantonese) or Zheng (in Mandarin), and spelled at the
whim of whomever was at the Immigration Desk as "Cheng" or "Jeng" or "Ja-
ang," was educated and lived in the far northern area of Ancient China. It was
important to be able to write the name in Chinese, which was the only way to
identify the person as a member of that family.

Because he was educated (he could read and write in Chinese, and had
studied history, mathematics, the sciences, literature, and could brush-paint and
write poetry) he was given the title of Mandarin by the Emperor and presided
over a community of tenants on land allotted to him.

He was in his early seventies when he was widowed, and his only offspring,
a daughter, had married and lived in the next village with her husband, father-
in-law and son. He had not seen them for some time, so one day he decided to
make the three-day trip to visit her. As he walked past the tenants on his land,

he was greeted happily by them and took the opportunity to stop for a cup of tea and a brief visit with each family.

Upon reaching his daughter's house, he became re-acquainted with his son-in-law, the son-in-law's father, and their little boy, who was just four years of age. He and his daughter's father-in-law sat and visited on the front porch while his daughter prepared dinner. Then the little boy appeared and said, "Grandpa, dinner is ready. Come now!" Old Mr. Chang responded, "Thank you. I will come now." The boy said, "I was not speaking to you. I was calling my Grandfather!" Lau Chang (old Chang) said, "I am your grandfather also," at which the four-year-old ran to his father's father, grabbing his leg, and said, "This is my grandfather. You are only a guest visiting and staying for dinner."

The fact that his grandson, who would someday inherit all his property, did not acknowledge him as grandfather, bothered him so much that he refused the invitation to spend the night and decided instead to make the long trek back to his home that evening. He knew he could find lodging at any one of his tenants' homes if he so wished.

Darkness was approaching and as he trudged along, he was met by one of his tenants, who invited him to stop and rest. Since he had not eaten much at his daughter's, he accepted the invitation to have dinner with the tenant's family. Immediately the tenant delegated his three daughters to prepare a special meal for Lau Chang, their landlord. ("Lau" is the respectful term to address a senior person.) One daughter slaughtered a chicken, drained the blood into a special container for future cooking, also separating the chicken parts, placing the bones in a pot of water to simmer, for broth. Another daughter gathered vegetables from their garden and quickly sliced them for steaming. The third daughter was to prepare the sauces for each dish but could not find space in the kitchen since both chopping blocks were in use and there was no cleaver available for her to smash the ginger.

Ingenuously, she placed the chunk of ginger on the hem of her Chinese-style blouse, folded the cloth over to protect the ginger, and brought it up to her mouth, crushing it with her teeth. She added other ingredients into a bowl to complete the sauce.

It was now dark and he was content, and happily accepted their invitation to spend the night and leave the next day for the long trek to his mansion on the distant hill.

When Lau Chang went to the bathroom, the tenant peeked and was happy to see that he was still "virile." The next morning, he broached the subject of his widowhood and his good health and suggested he should take on a wife and not end his years on earth alone and unattended. The tenant said, "I have three daughters, all well-trained by my wife in home duties. You could have your choice." The tenant also relished the idea of becoming a relative of his landlord. Lau Chang smiled and said, "I have not had a chance to think of a lonely future. You have put some ideas in my head." He also thought of his grandson who did not acknowledge him as his grandfather.

Then he said, "I like what you suggest, and your daughters are each so capable. I would like the 'geung chart,' the Ginger Crusher. I have seen her belly-button. It is round and full and means she is meant to have a comfortable life." (I have been informed that belly, or "bili," is short for "umbilicus.")

"The Ginger-Crusher? I do not know what you mean. Who showed you her belly-button? What a shame!!!"

Lau Chang responded, "No, not a shame. She was ingenuous. There was no room for her in the kitchen, so she found a way to crush the ginger. When she lifted the ginger in the hem of her blouse to her teeth, she unwittingly exposed her midriff, and I saw how beautifully formed and full was her 'too-chee' (belly-button)."

Lau Chang was also well-versed in phrenology, interpreting character and personality by physical attributes. Character and personality could be determined by the formation of cheekbones, the shape formed at the base of the neck, shape of the face, ankles, shape of the "too-chee," and so on.

The marriage was arranged. Since the "principal" wife had died, leaving no sons who would outrank her, the new wife had the honorable position of "First Wife," not "Second Wife" or Concubine. In the course of time she gave birth to seven sons, all of whom were fortunate to be able to be educated and who passed all the kingdom's examinations with flying colors. The emperor meanwhile faced with an expanding dominion and, wishing to unify it, made each of Lau Chang's sons a Mandarin, and sent them to different regions to become rulers (guides and protectors).

One was sent to the Shanghai Port Area, another to the far, far west by the Gobi Desert, another to the southwest Hunan area, one to the island country of Formosa (which we now know as Taiwan), one to Central China, and one to the northeast area near Korea. The oldest son remained in north, north China. The Chang brother (or son) who was my immediate ancestor was sent to Shensi Province, where several years ago around the city of Sian was unearthed several hundred soldiers fashioned with great artistic skill of ceramic clay, in full soldier regalia, with some civilian maids and servants.

The duty and responsibility of the position of Mandarin, or Scholar, required that new ideas leading to inventions improving quality of life be made each year and recorded for the education of future generations. Each of the seven sons are credited with remarkable discoveries. In the National Museum in Peking, which is now known to the modern world as Beijing, is an invention to detect the location and direction of an earthquake. It is a structure about two feet high with a marble ball in each of four corners, with a slot leading to the open mouth of a frog below in each corner. In the event of an earthquake, the structure will tip in the direction of its origin and the marble ball will slide down its slot into the open mouth of the frog below, thus indicating the area of concern.

In the sixteenth century, a Chang descendant defeated the "native army" of Formosa, now known as Taiwan, claiming the island for the Middle Kingdom. There is a statue to this ancestor in a park just outside the capital city of Taiwan. Another ancestor is credited with the creation of a product on which histories may be recorded, the mashing together of rice straws and pulp to create paper on which to write or draw.

Recently, on public TV, there was a documentary on a 15th century explorer from China, Zheng-He, who in 1421 sailed the world with a hundred ships and landed on parts of Central and South America. This indicates that the "New World" was "discovered" seventy-one years before Christopher Columbus arrived in 1492. It is surmised that the maps Columbus used were from Zheng-

He. In the art and lifestyle of modern-day Mexico and South America are many touches of a mingling of Chinese and South American art symbols.

In very rural southwestern China, in a crossroads where four towns meet, is a monument to the scholar who taught the residents agrarian skills to help them enjoy a more productive way of living "off the land."

Of course, I know best the story of an immediate ancestor who, perhaps accidentally but most fortuitously, discovered that two sticks can be used together at the dinner table to enable dining to be a pleasurable and not too messy activity...Chopsticks!!!

After my ancestor was re-assigned to the southern province of Canton, several generations ago his descendant incurred the wrath of the Emperor and he was deposed. No longer with the rank of Scholar and Mandarin, and no immediate way to earn a living, the ensuing poverty led to the selling of a daughter (for some immediate monetary relief), after which my father joined a boatload of Cantonese men to either go to Gold Mountain and "pick up the gold from the streets" there or to Sandalwood Mountain (Hawaii) to harvest the precious sandalwood, which is so prized for sandalwood incense for temple worship.

In the late 1930's a man arrived from China with *The Book of Chang,* which he wanted to supplement, knowing there were Changs who had left the Middle Kingdom. In this book was chronicled the many lines of Chang, with a special section for the "Too-Chee" (Belly-Button) Changs. We wanted to make copies of it. He would not let it out of his sight. Copying technique had not been developed yet, so we arranged meetings with him, which were cut short when he learned that the invading Japanese army was fast approaching his village and he rushed home to his family.

Since then, we have added to our history each time we meet someone descended from the seven original "too-chee" Changs. While at Oberlin College one summer, a professor with the same anglicized surname as I approached me and asked me to write my name in Chinese. Then he asked if I had a special story to my name. When I answered, "I'm a 'Too-Chee' Chang," he let out a whoop and said, "So am I!!! Come home and have dinner with my family!" Imagine meeting a "belly button" Chang in Ohio.

The descendants from the first Lau Chang are spread far and wide. They all seem to carry with them the primary priorities for the better life: education, community service, and outreach, and continuous personal development.

So far I have not been asked to show my belly button to justify my acknowledgement of my ancestry. My friends believe me. Those who don't believe me are not my friends.

Spring 2006

The Kitchen God

Fifteen days before the first day of the Chinese New Year, which changes each year because the Lunar Calendar is followed, brown sugar and molasses are rubbed on the lips of the Kitchen God. His picture has been hanging all year in a prominent place in the kitchen where he can view all the family goings-on…good, bad, happy, or squabbly). He is sent on his way (through fire) to the next world to, hopefully, give a sweet report of the family's activities of the past year.

If the report is not good, then the forecast for the upcoming year indicates difficulty and struggles with bringing happy events into everyday life. Usually the report is good and sweet, which foretells a prosperous and happy year to come. On New Year's Day a new Kitchen God is placed in that strategic place to observe and subsequently give a new report at the end of the coming year.

Meanwhile, preparations for the New Year continue: new outfits must be made or bought, and something new for the household is procured. All dusting and sweeping, and washing of hair and clothes are completed. Foods are prepared ahead of time so that there will be no need to cook on that FIRST DAY, and "red paper" money is prepared as gifts to family with the usual annual blessing.

We had a poignant experience in September 1976 brought on by the presence of the Kitchen God in my kitchen.

The war activities in Vietnam resulted in many families having to evacuate quickly, without any time or opportunity to prepare for such a hasty departure. Our church had indicated a wish to sponsor one family. Members of the church hastily found an apartment, and donations of furniture and other household necessities quickly came trailing in. Hearing that the head of the family spoke some English and had a driver's license, even an automobile was made available for the family's use.

I was in attendance at church the day the family was introduced to the congregation. Since I was the only person who looked Asian to them, at coffee time after the service they gravitated to me. The man and his wife had three young children, a girl about seven, and two boys about five and two. Impulsively, I invited them to have dinner with us that evening and gave them directions to our house.

They arrived early. In addition to the family they brought along her sister and her young child. Feeling the need to prepare more food for dinner, I went to the kitchen and added another pot of rice to cook and quickly sliced more vegetables and meat.

They followed me into the kitchen. Suddenly, I heard heated and intense conversation going on behind me. As I turned around to see what was causing the commotion, the man said to me in his faltering English, "My wife sees the Kitchen God above the stove and wants to know if you are Buddhist." When I told him I had been brought up in Hawaii and observed Buddhist, Taoist, and Confucian principles, he said to me, with deep, controlled emotion, "We had to leave Viet Nam so suddenly. We were not able to gather spiritual mementos. We just have what we could carry for our personal needs. We don't even know what day this is on the Lunar Calendar!"

He paused briefly and, with obvious (to me) controlled emotion, asked, "When is Moon Festival Day? My wife sees your Kitchen God, your big knife (cleaver), and the log that is your cutting board. The church friends supplied us with many useful household things. We have three lounge chairs, two beds, and something they call a Rice Pot. It does not cook rice like you are cooking now. We do not know how to use it."

Hearing that, I could hardly control my own emotions. I pulled out my Chinese calendar, which he could read because the Chinese influence is very strong there, since China once claimed Viet Nam as their Southern province (Nam means South in Chinese), and he was part Chinese. As he spread the news to his wife and her sister that they had not missed Moon Festival Day, I said, "I can take your wife to San Francisco next Saturday to purchase what equipment you need that is familiar to you." In 1976, there were no stores in San Mateo that carried Chinese cooking needs and only two Chinese restaurants. (You know that is different now.)

The next Saturday I drove to their apartment. The whole family (including her sister and her child) piled in. They all wanted to see San Francisco. This was before mandatory seat belts. I drove them to Chinatown and led them to my favorite housewares stores. In addition to cooking pots they recognized, they purchased chopsticks, rice bowls, baskets for steaming, and a calendar that showed Lunar Calendar dates and observances. We had a special lunch in a Chinese restaurant.

Returning to San Mateo, I was absolutely exhausted, but it was a delicious type of fatigue. I could not imagine myself suddenly in a foreign country, trying to understand what people were saying, and not being able to find familiar foods and vegetables for my family.

At their apartment they expressed their gratitude and wanted me to stay for dinner. At my refusal, I told them how much their presence in my life had enriched my understanding of people's personal needs, not tangible THINGS, but the intangible cultural observances that enhance our daily experiences.

All this because they saw the Kitchen God in my kitchen and realized we shared a common faith and trust in customs that span generations into the past.

The Importance of
Chinese Tea Ceremonies

Many tea ceremonies are observed by Chinese families, with variations and adjustments to account for changing customs and times. Because of a deep appreciation of this time-tested ancestral heritage, these parents hope that the younger generation will also learn to appreciate and be aware of their heritage. There is a book entitled *CHA-CHING, The Classic of Tea* to elevate tea and tea-drinking to its unique place as the symbol of veneration in Chinese society. Of course, time brings changes, and there must be modifications reasonably compatible with modern trends of behavior, or else rituals and traditions may be abandoned.

Tea has been identified as a beverage integral to the Chinese spirit, and the act of tea drinking as a celebration of life. Each tea hour becomes a masterpiece to serve as a distillation of all tea hours, as if it were the first with no other to follow, according to *Cha-Ching*, the classic written by scholar Lu Yu around 760 CE.

Many couples of Chinese extraction still observe the tradition of the bridal tea ceremony on their wedding day. Many young couples feel, as do their parents, that a cup of sweetened tea symbolizes the essence of life, so on their great day of happiness they wish to share this sweetness and joy with their relatives and dear friends.

Much of the Chinese behavior is influenced by Confucian ideals. Then, too, there are two fundamental thoughts. Ancestor worship takes care of the past and deeply reflects filial piety (respect for parents and elders), which takes care of the present. This has continued for generations.

Actually there were two tea ceremonies in the traditional Chinese wedding, one held on the morning the bride leaves her home to go to her in-law's home, and the other occurring at the bridegroom's. Since practically all Americans of Chinese ancestry favor a church wedding today, the tea ceremony is usually held as part of the wedding reception, or immediately after the reception at a private residence, banquet hall, or hotel.

For the bridal tea ceremony, a specially decorated table stands in full view. On it there is a display of fresh fruits like pomelos, oranges, and tangerines, a sweetened sticky cake or "gao," and, most important, candied fruits.

Everything on the table represents great blessings. The pomelos and oranges symbolize the greater types of good luck, while the tangelos represent the lesser kinds of good luck. The "gao" is sweet, in keeping with the sweet life. It also means advancement to the heights, with a stick-to-it attitude in case the advancement might at times be slow. Beside the decorated table is another table on which beautiful Chinese teapots, teacups, and saucers sit with a huge plate of candied fruits cut into strips.

The performance of the bridal tea ceremony itself—a fitting symbol for the memorable occasion—is next. Since most of the customs originated from Canton, which is my parental origin, and where most of the Chinese in Hawaii are from, the bride usually changes to a "cheong-sam." ("Cheong" means LONG; "sam" means ITEM OF CLOTHING.) She enters resplendent in a red or black silk jacket, embroidered in gold or with multicolor and silver. In the old days, the bride is assisted by the go-between, but in this day and age, she is assisted by her maid-of-honor or a close friend. She goes around pouring tea for her new in-laws and relatives. For the bridal cup of tea, candied fruit is added as she receives a generous "li-see," or money wrapped in red paper, from each person, with best wishes and good luck. After the first round, the bride pours for everyone for a second time for added good luck.

The tea-pouring ceremony generally follows the tradition, serving the new in-laws first, then the bride's own family. For each generation, the male is always served first, before the female.

For our wedding, I made some adjustments to meet the needs of my new extended family.

2 October 2013.   .

Myth of The Seventh Sister

Every several weeks throughout the year, our family trekked to the home of AH PO, my maternal grandmother, for an observance and celebration of ancestors, mythical gods or goddesses, who were the source of our blessings, or just an excuse for feasting and fun.

Mama was one of eight, and among each family's offspring sprouted thirty-one first cousins. I was in the lower third, age wise, so I did not have much to do with food preparation for these monthly gatherings, but was involved with set-up and clean-up.

We would gather around AH PO, and she, or one of her sons or daughters, would tell the story of the festival we were observing. One of my favorites was of the Spinning Maid and the Cowherd. It was explained that in China, farmers raised water buffaloes (referred to as water cows) to assist in the care of the crops on their land.

As she looked up at the clear sky Ah Po told the story that we had heard from birth each summer:

"According to legend," she began, "the Emperor of Heaven had seven daughters, all skilled in what was often referred to as 'feminine skills.'" These skills included food preparation, house arrangement, singing, dancing, storytelling, and fabric enhancement, which included weaving, embroidering, crocheting, and lace making. The youngest daughter, his seventh child, was especially gifted in spinning and weaving the finest silk, the smoothest cloth, and imparting intricate designs on the fabrics she wove.

One day, the seven sisters descended to earth to bathe in a steam near a green pasture. A handsome young man was tending his water cow by the side of a stream. He was fond of the huge black beast which drew the plow for him, and he took care to lead her where the greenest grass grew and where there was water deep enough for her to wallow to her heart's content.

As the youth lay on the grassy bank beside the grazing cow, he saw the maidens relaxing in the pristine water and stood up, enchanted by their beauty. He noticed six were swimming as a group, and the seventh was by herself on the other side of the stream.

The water cow was a fairy beast with the power of talking, and as the young man looked in wonder at the seven maidens, she spoke:

"Those are maidens from the Heavenly Kingdom. The six who swim there as a group are well enough, but the one by herself on the other side of the stream is the wisest of them all. She spins thread and makes cloth for the gods, softer than the softest cloud, and with the colors of the most brilliant sunset. Hide her red robe, that one by the yonder stone. Without it she cannot fly back to the sky. She will have to remain here on earth, and you will be able to marry her."

When the seven maids had finished their swimming, six put on their robes and rode away to the sky on the backs of white cranes. The seventh, the fair spinning maid, could not find her robe and was forced to stay behind. When the young cowherd stepped forward with her robe gently draped over his arm, she quickly took her silk covering and threw it over her shoulders. She found the young man so handsome, so kind, and so good. Her grateful eyes met his. Her heart told her she had just met her soulmate, and she decided to remain on earth with him.

The couple married, and for three years nothing happened to disturb them. Two beautiful children brought light to their household. Under their roof love and joy reigned. So immersed were they in each other, the lovers began to neglect their talents and responsibilities. The weaving maiden ceased her needlework and the cowherder ignored his livestock.

In the Heavenly Kingdom no soft silken garments came from the loom which the spinning maid left behind her. The Queen Mother of the West, the Heavenly Mother, angry at all this negligence, demanded that she, the Weaving Maiden, return home. As a daughter of the heavens, she obeyed, sacrificing her own happiness. She retrieved her heavenly silk garments and ascended to the sky.

The cowherder attempted to follow her, but was not able to reach his beloved. When the Sun God heard of the forced separation, he was immensely saddened. Out of compassion, he allowed the couple to meet each year for a week, beginning on the seventh day of the seventh moon on the lunar calendar.

Each year, in the constellation with seven stars, only six are visible. I have often wondered what constellation that is until I learned that the group of seven stars is called the Pleiades, and for several weeks every summer only six are visible. Could the missing one be the seventh sister visiting her earthly mortal husband?

Each year on this memorable night, gallon jugs are filled with water, representing the tears of joy the couple shed as they meet again after a year's absence. This water will keep for a long time without becoming murky and is used on special occasions, as brewing special tea for visitors or for steeping medicinal herbal brews, or for soups on special occasions. Mama faithfully filled six gallons of water at midnight each year.

Some years ago, after Mama left this planet, as we were dismantling her home, we came across six jugs of water in a special closet. Mama usually filled them each year at the proper time, the water representing the tears of joy and love (called "Hoakai Tsui") in anticipation of the annual reunion of the lovers. However, during WWII when Hawaii went on daylight savings time, Mama wanted to be sure to touch all bases, so she filled six at midnight on daylight savings time, and six more when she considered it "regular" time.

One brother said "toss them," but brother #2, who had a great sense of tradition, directed me to prepare some broth and velvet chicken and a delicious kind of herbal soup, using the special water in memory of Mama's special devotion to legends.

Even today, I observe some of these treasured traditions, although the person I live with, a Barbarian who had a different mother, tells me that pure water can be obtained from the market in sealed bottles. I gently remind him that I learned to place a cookie and a glass of milk for Santa, and I annually hunt for colored Easter eggs left by the Easter bunny.

Because of the treasured skills in so-called feminine activities, this festival honors women who excel to some degree. Each year on the day before the seventh day of the seventh moon, a maiden will float a needle in a glass of water, and the shadow cast from the needle is analyzed. If the shadow looks like a leaf or a flower, the maiden will be highly proficient, but if the shadow resembles a stick, she should seek work in the kitchen.

Also, a spider is placed in a small wooden box on the evening of "seven/seven," or the Double Seventh Festival, Chinese Valentine's Day. If the spider has been productive during the night, spinning with form and shape, it was an omen for great success as a master seamstress. If not, it means more work and study for the young girl. It was not until I was sixteen that a spider spun a beautiful web for me. By then, I could crochet, knit, applique, sew, and weave, and I was delirious with joy. However, I do not do this anymore; why be in danger of changing the verdict? Besides, any creature with less than or more than two legs bothers me, so why chase down a spider anymore?

This is one of many myths or legends observed by my clan in Honolulu, memories that my maternal grandmother recalled from her childhood. Most of these stories develop because people want to give a reason for the celebrations throughout the year.   July 2008.

Moon Cakes and the Mid-Autumn Festival

My memory of our many family and clan gatherings always centered around stories of occasions in Chinese history to honor and remember, and symbolic foods to commemorate each event.

One of the most important and colorful holidays is the Moon Festival, which is celebrated on the fifteenth day of the eighth month on the Chinese Lunar Calendar. The day differs each year, since the calculation of the first day of each year is made by division of the moon cycles. The observation is that it also coincides with Harvest Festivals of other ethnic groups, such as the Jewish Sukkoth.

Preparation for this day, and for two weeks after, included decorating the household with signs of a prosperous harvest. In addition to flowers, bowls of fresh fruit (especially those that are round) and vegetables were displayed that could be eaten immediately, or preserved for the winter.

The moon shines brightest on this day—big and round and vividly orange.

Each year the following story is told:

One day, in the Shia Dynasty, the Son of Heaven, riding forth from his palace in a sedan chair, saw upon the highway a man with long arrows and a huge red bow in his hands. The Emperor had never seen another bow like it, and he stopped to examine it.

In response to the Emperor's question, the man replied, "I am Wen Hou Ye. With my taut bow I shoot arrows from one side of the world to the other. I ride on the winds. I am lighter than air since I eat only flowers."

The Emperor was astonished. He hardly believed these words of Hou Ye. He said, "Do you see yonder the pine tree on the top of that distant mountain? Send an arrow through its branches. If you can do that, we shall give you the post of Imperial Archer."

Hou Ye took aim. He bent his red bow and, straight as the bird flies, his arrow sped to the pine tree on the top of that far mountain. At once the bowman jumped upon the passing wind and flew off to fetch a branch from that tree.

The emperor kept his promise. Hou Ye was named Imperial Archer. Again and again, Hou Ye was called upon to aim his red bow at some enemy—at wicked animals, clouds that would not rain, floods, and enemy armies. He became so famous that the Ho Po, the great God of the Waters, offered his beautiful sister Cheng-O to be his bride.

Not long after, a dreadful thing happened. In the sky there appeared not one, but ten round burning disks which sent their fierce rays down on the earth. Leaves died on their branches; grass blades burned to a crisp. No grain could grow. In the terrible heat the water dried up in the wells, as did the streams. Quickly, the Emperor called for Hou Ye.

"O, Archer," he said. "We need you to save us. The soothsayers say that in each sun lives a golden raven on whose life the sun's heat and light depends. Take your red bow and shoot the gold ravens, or we shall all die."

Hou Ye drew back his bow and aimed it at the sky. Zing-ng-ng went his arrow as it flew straight and sure to the first of the blazing suns. Zing-ng-ng, a second arrow was dispatched upward to find the second sun; three, four, five, six, seven, eight, nine ravens were killed by the arrows of Hou Ye.

As Hou Ye was taking aim at the tenth raven, a voice came from the clouds. "Hold on, Archer," it said. "Listen to me. I am the Sun God. Leave one sun in the sky so that the earth may be lighted. Without its brightness and warmth no one could live. Take care how you shoot." Hou Ye stayed his hand, and the tenth sun still shines, high up there in the heavens.

Hou Ye's fame spread far and wide. The Empress of the West heard of this good deed and ordered that Hou Ye be brought before her. She presented him with the Pill of Long Life.

"When you swallow this, Mighty Archer, you shall be carried to the heavens where you will live forever. But do not swallow it now; the time is not ready. For twelve months you must prepare yourself. Hide the pill away. Keep it a secret until the hour comes for you to fly away to the sky."

When Hou Ye returned home, he followed the Imperial instructions and hid the Pill of Long Life high in the ceiling. He told no one, not even his wife.

Soon after that came a directive from the Emperor. He was needed in the south to deal with a crisis there.

Cheng-O found the time waiting for her husband very long. One day, she noticed a bright light high up in the corner near the roof. Sweet perfume filled the air. She climbed the ladder and found the pearly white pill. While still on the ladder, she heard Hou Ye's footsteps approaching the front door. *Hou Ye is home!* she thought. *He will be angry if he sees me with this pill.* She quickly put it in her mouth as he entered the door. As Hou Ye said, "What are you doing up there?" Cheng-O's body became light, and her body flew out the window, up towards the sky. Hou Ye ran after her, calling "Cheng-O, stop! Come back!" but she was powerless in the force of the pill.

When Cheng-O reached the moon, she landed with a thump. Out from her mouth flew the shell of the pill, which immediately became a rabbit of the purest white jade. A part of the pill turned into a cassia tree (from which we get the spice cinnamon), and Cheng-O became a toad, but just for a short time. She sat beautifully under the cassia tree and next to the rabbit, glowing as the harvest moon.

As this story was told to us each year, we feasted on the fruits of the Harvest and enjoyed the moon cakes that have become a part of the story. Often, a spontaneous lantern parade would develop, and we shook lighted sparklers towards the moon as we chanted the Moon Festival rhyme.

Originally, the cakes were made with sweetened, fermented black beans with the yolk of a duck's egg in the center (to imitate the large, orange harvest moon in a dark sky). There was a time when the cakes were hollow and used to send messages to others of clandestine meetings, i.e. "Meet me at 9PM at Jake's barn." In the century when Kubla Khan of the Han Dynasty ruled, warring groups planning aggressive strategies would call for secret meetings, the location and time inserted in a hollowed-out moon cake.

Since the traditional Moon Cake of a duck egg yolk, surrounded by sweetened, fermented black beans, requires much accommodation—a truly acquired taste—other fillings have been devised, such as winter melon, orange peel and black sugar, loquats, lotus, and such.

In past years bakeries with this special cake would close the day before Moon Festival Day so that employees may observe this special day at home or with relatives. Now, the tourist trade has become more aware of the special taste and meaning of this significant day, and moon cakes are available year-round, especially with the new flavor combinations created to please the western palate.

Cakes are to be made one by one. The delicate, fine dough is pressed into the sides and bottom of a round mold, which has symbols of the hare, toad, and cassia tree etched into the bottom and sides. Then, the fillings are tightly packed in and a topping placed on the open spaces. After removal from the mold, the cake is then baked.

As a young child we never looked for the "Man in the Moon" or the cow jumping over the moon. We knew that the moon was not made of green cheese. We looked for the Moon Lady, or Goddess, who always smiled down at us as we lit sparklers and chanted the rhyme to the moon, which is, in part:

> ngit gong gong
> giu de tong
> nien sahn mahn
> ja but long

In twelve more lunar months this festival will re-occur and we will remember and honor the story of the Imperial Archer Hou Ye and Cheng-O, the Moon Goddess, and her flight to the moon.

Preparing Holy Money

As the youngest in a large family, my earliest memory of "school days" was that of my brothers traipsing off to school while I remained at home with my mother because I was not yet of "school age." After wandering about a bit, I would seek her out. She was always involved in a project and, upon seeing me, would include me in what she was working on.

If she was working on looping long bias strips into cords to be formed into Chinese buttons, she would quickly prepare a short strip for me, fashion a small thimble for me from a scrap of leather, and hand me a threaded needle. I proudly sat by her side, working on what I considered a "grown-up" project. Or, if the project that day was turning collars and cuffs on Papa's white shirts, she taught me how to rip the seams and baste the "good" side back on the shirt.

Every several days she would appear all dressed up in a certain corner of the living room used for entertaining visitors, near the altar where incense was offered to the pictured Gods and Goddesses, and the display of fruits, flowers, and pomelo leaves in water.

On the table were two stacks of fine rice paper, a bit larger than a five-inch square. In the center of one pile was a two-inch square of gold; in the middle of the other stack, a silver square.

Relatives who have departed this planet need help to continue living graciously in the next world. Objects (clothes, a car, furniture) usually made in miniature of bamboo or fabric are sent to them on certain feast days so that they may continue to live comfortably. These are sent through fire.

Money is most necessary to give them status. But money is not thrown carelessly into the Holy Furnace to be transported to beloved relatives in their new environment. Each item of cash is folded and attached. The minimum amount sent is usually one thousand, which takes a while to fold. So some money is folded each week in anticipation of a future need.

As Mama proceeded to teach me the intricate folds, which were difficult at first for my small fingers, I began to feel uplifted as I realized I was taking part in an activity involving another world.

"First," Mama cautioned me, "be sure your hands and clothes are clean, and you are thinking only good thoughts. Then, pick up one piece of money, fold it in half, but do NOT crease the center line. Fold the two ends together tightly. Press in the ends at an angle, so now you have a rounded trapezoid. Curve the two pointed ends up into the shape of a boat. The square of gold, or silver, is now in the center. Now, fold ten before we stop for morning tea and fruit."

At Tea Time I had only completed three. Mama said we would spend a short time practicing the folds each day. I enjoyed having tea and fruit with Mama. I felt like a grown-up as we selected a piece of fruit from our garden, either papaya, avocado, banana, orange, or apple.

It took me several days before I could complete ten before Tea Time. I learned to count to ten in Chinese. One day I folded ten and three more. Mama taught me to count in Chinese: "Ten and one is eleven; ten and two is twelve…" and so on. As I lined the second row of three under the first row, she asked me how many more would I need to match the first row. I counted out seven. "Three and seven equals ten!" I shrieked. Each day this occurred with different combinations of numbers…to equal ten. She was exposing me to Base Ten Arithmetic before I could even write the numbers, in Chinese or in English!!!

One day she handed me a six-inch needle (like those used in making flower leis), threaded with light string and taught me to connect ten without piercing the paper, creating a round flower. She placed this in a large basket. After some time, I had strung ten bundles of ten and had a hundred pieces of money, some with gold centers and some with silver, which I connected into one large bundle.

On the next Feast Day, she took me to the Temple with the thousand she had folded, and my hundred, and offered it to the Priest proudly. The Priest accepted both bundles, ceremoniously placing them in the Holy Urn for the relative we were honoring, and sending the Holy Money on its way.

Thirty-five years later, as I folded the thousand for my father at the celebration of his life, and sixteen years after that, for my mother, the memory of my first accomplishment before I was five permeated my thoughts and eased the accompanying thoughts of physical separation, and instead strengthened the bonds of tradition instilled in me at a very early age.

In 1959, we moved to San Mateo for continuing employment in Social Work and Education. On weekends I explored the thirty-four square blocks of San Francisco Chinatown and visited the many Chinese temples there. I found one that was Buddhist AND Taoist, on Portsmouth Square, above the parking structure at Kearny and Washington. The priests and priestesses spoke my Cantonese dialect. I was welcomed there and attended many festival functions. I was able to prepare Holy Money there on Feast Days to send to departed relatives. In recent years when bruises and physical limitations from several accidents and falls limited my excursions to San Francisco, I registered my parents' names. Now I give money annually so someone on their staff will prepare "holy money" to send (through fire) to insure the continuing comfort of my parents in their current world.

Although I am now physically unable to participate in the various activities of the temples, experiences learned as a young child are vivid memories that I cherish and are added to current "Christian" observances that surround me now.

April 2011

Sayings from the Sages

I was not read to as a child; I was talked to and sung to, which gave special authority to the lesson involved. To lend strength and credence to the lesson, the source was usually Confucious, Buddha, or Lao Tsu, or one of the helpers of Buddha.

To maintain good health (with vitality and enjoyment), special herb brews were prepared on a regular basis. Some were prescribed by an herbalist, and others were "common" everyday concoctions that Mama remembered from her mother. Since she had not been taught how to read or write, she knew them from memory.

Every week Mama would drive to Honolulu to her favorite herbalist. Since I was the only one at home during the day (my older brothers were in school), I went along with her. Often, when there was no parking on the busy street, she would double park and send me to tell the herbalist which prescription she needed for that day.

There was one particular package she always ordered that was a non-prescription concoction she brewed weekly as a general tonic for the family. There were nine ingredients. Mama recited them to me so I could request them from the herbalist.

It was a difficult combination for me to remember. I would run in and call respectfully to the herbalist the package that Mama wanted that day. I panted, "Wai sahn, lin gee, bahk hop, ee gee…" Then I would pause and wail, "I can't remember the five more things."

The man would peer out of the store window, see my mother waving her hands, and say to me, "Don't worry, I see your mother. I know what she always orders." And he quickly measured out the nine ingredients and packaged them. I gave him the coins and ran out to the car just before a policeman reached Mama to tell her to "Move on; no double parking here."

At home, Mama would place the contents of this valuable package into a huge pot with water and a hunk of meat (for flavor) to stew for several hours. This was a flavorful soup that was not bitter as some medicinal broths are. I liked it, especially since I was told it was necessary to maintain good health. After drinking it, we were each given one of the six golden raisins the herbalist always included, wrapped up in a small package as a reward for ingesting the medicinal qualities of this tonic.

There were other herbal brews that Mama ordered, some by prescription from a certified herbal doctor, others she remembered from her mother's teachings. Specifically, there was a monthly concoction she steeped just for me, for females, that was not very tasty and hard to stomach. I wonder if this horrible tasting medicine is the reason I never suffered any monthly discomfort, and gave birth without the legendary labor pains. I wish I could remember what went into that brew.

When it became apparent that I had difficulty remembering which item of food preparation required garlic and which required ginger, or both, since it was important that at least one dish each day should have ginger, or garlic, or both, Mama recited a verse she had been taught, the better to help me remember. To prepare herself to educate me, she straightened her back, leaned back slightly, and spoke, almost mechanically, in a most reverent tone, as if the voice of a sage or her mother were speaking through her:

"Hin choi, dow miu, gai-lan, chow SIN GEE," roughly translated as, "When preparing spinach, Chinese eggplant, potato, dow miu, kelp, Chinese broccoli, or mustard cabbage, sauté at least two to four minced cloves of garlic in hot oil before adding vegetables to pan."

"Doh-fu, ker gai-choi, look-dow, chow GEUNG." Sauté mashed GINGER in hot oil before adding tofu, radishes, yams, tomato, Job's tears, fava beans, Chinese broccoli, and mustard Cabbage to pan.

"Look-dow, gai-choi, ngee, chow GEUNG ho SIN GEE." Some may be enhanced by both ginger and garlic, such as string beans, Job's tears, mustard cabbage, and fish.

There is also a chant the sages sang through Mama on how to tell when seafood is done, ready to be served:

"Ngee dut ngan," meaning fish eyes balloon out (indicating the complete fish, with head still attached, is prepared and ready to be served in its entirety).

"Hai loong eeu" (shrimp or prawn: the spine curves).

"Hah hoong hawk" (crab or lobster: the shell turns red).

The above, when recited in Chinese prose, is quite melodic. You can see that the chant loses its rhythm and beauty in translation.

One day, when I was about ten years of age, as I was chopping and slicing vegetables and meat on the tree trunk slab which was my chopping board, I cut my hand near the thumb. As Mama was applying pressure on the incision to stem the flow of blood, she said, (quoting from the sages, I thought), "The knife, made of steel, is an inanimate object. You, a human being, are animate and able to control items not blessed with life. One should always be in control, and not let an inanimate object get the best of you."

That lesson, that thought, stayed with me for decades. Whenever I held the Chinese cleaver and sliced and chopped away (which was several times daily), I had the unconscious/conscious thought that I am in control of this inanimate object. Four and a half decades later, when I was fifty-five years of age, the cleaver I was using slipped on the slick skin of a solid fruit and gashed my hand. As I was stemming the flood of blood, I began to scream and sob in a flow of tears. Bob rushed in to hear me shout, "If you ever meet my mother in the next world, don't ever tell her that I let that inanimate object get the best of me."

Not knowing the story of my lesson as a ten-year-old, he calmly said, "It's not a big deal. Here, let me apply pressure to stem the flow of blood."

I screamed, "You don't understand!" Then, as I calmed down a bit, I realized that he did not understand, not knowing the history of my early escapade at age ten with an inanimate object.

It seems that every day a situation would occur that would elicit a quotation, a wise saying from some ancient scholar or sage, leading to a lesson to be learned to simplify the rigors of daily life. Although I felt these wise sayings reflected the teaching techniques of my parents, they always gave credit to the ancient sage or scholar they were quoting.

After three arranged marriages for me did not happen, I went away to college. I never met the young men to whom I was engaged. They were much older than me and chose to marry someone closer to their age and of their choice. Upon completion of my studies, I chose to remain in California for one year before returning home to Honolulu, or so I thought. One day I called my parents to announce, "Mama, Papa, somebody wants to marry me!"

Initially they may have thought, "Grab him!" but Mama calmly asked, "What is his name?" When I said "Bob Wilkinson," I knew they thought this name did not sound Chinese, but Mama said, "Does he measure up to the qualities one looks for in a future mate?"

Another question from the sages, two thoughts only, but all encompassing: "Yau sum" literally means "has heart," meaning thoughtful and considerate.

"Yau boon gee": resourceful, able to provide

I said, "Yes, yes." I did not tell them that he was just out of the war (World War II) and attending UC Berkeley on the GI Bill, which was about to expire.

These are some incidents in my life controlled and sometimes directed by teachings and questions of the Ancients. In retrospect, I wish that I could have lived closer to my parents when we were raising our children and passed on more of the wise sayings that infused my life.

2009

Words of Wisdom

Growing up in a Chinese family, we were often taught by proverbs and sayings. For example, once, when I got word that we were having unexpected company, I scurried about the house picking up after my four children. As I was moaning about the condition of the house, I was told, "Don't worry about what the house looks like. A messy house is a happy house, because you know there are children around." That made my day.

Another time, out of the blue, our kitchen was invaded by huge carpenter ants. They hung around for days. The whole house was in an uproar, except for Goong-Goong (grandfather). He advised, "Just feed them, and they'll go away." That night we scattered bread crumbs all over the kitchen floor. Next morning, lo and behold, the ants were gone and they never came back.

My maternal grandmother used to say, "Feed your dogs at night and your cats in the morning. If the dogs are full, they'll stay at home to guard your house at night. But if you feed the cats at night, they won't catch the mice because they're not hungry."

We were also taught by quotations and/or sayings, which we found were also from other ethnic groups, such as:

"It is man that makes truth great, and not truth that makes man great."

"When drinking water, think of the source."

"Time flies as fast as an arrow."

"An ounce of gold can't buy an inch of time."

"In the wink of an eye, a year goes by."

"Give him an inch, he wants a foot."

"There is a beginning and there is an ending.
When you start something, you should finish it."

"Do unto others what you want others to do unto you."

"Simple family fare or every day food."

"Where there is a will, there is a way."

"Ten thousand things will be as you wish."

"Whatever is needed, there is available."

"The price is cheap, but the quality is good."

"When in China, do as the Chinese do."

You will note that these sayings are similar to quotations from ethnic books and/or the Holy Bible.   13 June 2012

Fish Heads, The Ultimate Delicacy

As a lowly girl-child growing up in a male-dominated society, one of the few pleasures—highlights in my life—was my turn to have the fish head to enhance my dinner.

Growing up in the Depression Era, in pre-World War II Wahiawa, a small rural town twenty-two miles from Honolulu and a mile from Schofield Barracks, our life was such that I did not know we were poor. Our needs were always met. I wore hand-me-down clothing, and there was always food on the table.

Once a week the highlight of dinner was a whole fish, steamed with salted black beans crushed with garlic and peanut oil, sliced ginger, green onions, and a dash of soyu sauce. We all took turns on who would have the fish head, which was also considered "brain food," to help in case there was a big examination coming up at school.

It seemed that, whenever it was my turn, a guest would arrive, or a brother would drop in from Honolulu where he was attending the University of Hawaii, and I would have to give up my turn for this prized delicacy.

The fish head was special. The round piece under each flap was often reserved for children. It was boneless, and so-o delicious. Then to suck on the eyes, and slurp up the brains from the channel, and a chance to play marbles later with the eyeballs.

I lost my turn so often, and complained so loudly about it, that every so often my mother would somehow procure a fish head JUST FOR ME, which I enjoyed without having to share it.

When I came to California, fish was never sold intact. It was always missing the head, which I learned later was thrown away. Only in Chinese markets could I find a fish with head and tail not separated from the body.

A few months after we were married and living in Berkeley, one day Bob came home from a fishing trip with two fish. He announced that he was cooking dinner that night, and he would cook the fish that he had caught. Great, I thought, and waited eagerly and hungrily for dinner to be served.

When he brought the fish to the table, both heads were missing. I was quite upset. I did not dare say anything. I had been taught to never, or almost never, correct another woman's son. Somehow I was able to get through dinner. I thought, *Is this love? He had eaten both heads by himself in the kitchen!!!* I had been taught not to show any unhappiness, but all I could think was that I had again lost my turn at a fish head to another man.

The next morning, while preparing breakfast, I opened the garbage can to discard some waste and saw the two fish heads there. Bob had thrown them away!!! He had not eaten them by himself in the kitchen last night!!! He had not been raised properly to enjoy the value and delight of fish heads!!! Poor boy!!!

Sometime later, we decided to make a trip to Honolulu for my family to meet Bob and our new baby. My parents were not able to come to our wedding in Berkeley. They were both too ill to make the trip. An aunt and uncle had come to represent them at the wedding and two of my brothers. They returned with glowing reports of Bob's family.

On the plane trip over (this was before jets, and it took nine and a half hours), I was anxious that Bob would act Barbarian and not show good manners and family training. I stressed, "Stand up to receive your first cup of tea. With both hands. And do not ask for a fork and ice water at the table." And on and on. I also knew that, since I was the one returning home, and I was bringing a husband and a GRANDSON for them, that there would be at dinner the ceremonial fish, with head and tail intact, for ME.

My parents were so charmed by Bob (he is more INSCRUTABLE than I am), that at dinner as the "piece de resistance" was brought to the table, my father broke off the head and, to indicate acceptance of him into the family, my father placed the head on his plate, with fish eyes looking straight up at him. My first reaction was selfish. I thought, *I have lost out again to a man.* HE was getting the fish head, not ME!! Then I noticed the look of shock and pain on Bob's face (which was also turning green) and thought, *He is in shock.* So, in my most formal, tactful Chinese, I explained to my father that Bob, brought up in Barbarian ways, had not been taught to enjoy the finer things at the table, and had not been schooled in the values and benefits of the fish head.

Quickly, my father understood, and said in pidgin English, "So, solly, Mr. Bob. So solly." They insisted on calling him MISTER Bob, and could only pronounce Bob as Bop. Then he placed the next most important part of the fish on Bob's plate, the STOMACH. As Bob hesitated, I snarled out of the side of my mouth, "Eat it!" which he did and discovered he enjoyed it.

The next day there was a gathering at the house of one of my brother's, with all the relatives and first cousins. There were about a hundred people there. Two cousins had spent the morning deep-sea fishing, and brought their catch to be smoked and otherwise prepared and served. Bob was enjoying a very succulent and delicious hors d'oeuvres and asked what it was. When he was told by this cousin that it was raw squid that he had caught that morning, and he had spent hours pounding it in the salt water of the ocean, Bob nearly choked on it. But he decided that, since he had enjoyed it so much before he knew what it was, he could continue to enjoy it.

Needless to say, Bob passed muster and was wholeheartedly accepted into the family, even though he had a Barbarian up-bringing.

One of the advantages I have living with someone not brought up to enjoy some of the "finer specialties of Chinese cuisine," is that, through the years, I have not had to share these "pieces de resistance" of food with anyone, and could have them all to myself. Some years later, here in San Mateo at a progressive dinner at which the main course was at our house, I told this story as an example of cultural adjustments people have to make occasionally. I also mentioned I had to learn to eat artichokes, cottage cheese, and mince pie.

When I completed my fish head story, a nice-looking well-bred (it seemed to me) man said, in an obviously intense and sincere outburst, "Gee, I'm glad I'm not married to you!" His wife quickly admonished, "Bill!!!" Noting his emotional manner, like one of relief, I thought, *How do I respond to that?* I only said, meekly and hopefully in a polite way, "I'm glad, too."

Years later, at the Chinese wedding banquet of one of our daughters, I had an experience which climaxed and partially ended my subservience to men. It is a custom in our family that at large banquets where there are many people seated at many tables, a member of the family would be assigned to each table. As each new course is served, each family member would then pick up his plate, rice bowl, chopsticks, and teacup, and move to the next table so that each guest would then have the opportunity to visit with all members of the host family.

On this particular occasion (a nine-course banquet), the whole steamed fish arrived at the table I had just moved to, at which sat one brother and his family who had flown in from Honolulu for the wedding and festivities. My brother's wife knew of the turmoil I always experienced over whose turn it was for the fish head. She said, with chuckles and laughter, "Now, who gets the fish head!" I quietly said, "Of course, Gordon gets it!" My brother Gordon nobly said, "No. You get it. We are at the banquet celebrating your daughter's marriage. You are the honored mother of the bride."

At last. Not age, but event, had awarded me with preference for the ultimate delicacy. And this from not only a male, but an older brother.

Each day I still experience "cultural conflicts," both due to occasions, or a search for the correct word or words in English. But the conflicts are no longer conflicts; instead they are opportunities for understanding how differently each person experiences life.

The Power of Three

From the very beginning of my conscious memory, the number three (3) seemed to be present in most "outward-appearing" household and family activities, a controlling factor in decision-making involving daily events.

You have heard that on the day I was born, at 8:00 in the morning, my father brought home from a shopping spree three (3) items meant to enhance and enrich my growing-up years and after:

#1. A mirrored vanity chest to assist me in my daily grooming activities before I left my bedroom each morning;

#2. A Moon Harp, sometimes called a Butterfly Harp, for daily family cultural and musical enrichment; and

#3. A large marble slab on which to create light, flaky Chinese pastries.

No more than three (3) match-marriages may be arranged. After being jilted three (3) times, that's IT. I was on my own, destined to prepare for my own future. No more than three (3) attempts can be made before one becomes an object of pity by the community.

P.S. I did find someone (on my own), not arranged by an official matchmaker, who was brave enough—had the courage—to take me on for a lifetime.

Three (3) essential and necessary tools accompany the bride into her new life:

#1. A Chinese cleaver to slice, chop, mash, or roll-cut, necessary skills in the art of meal preparation;

#2. Chopsticks, a pair about fifteen inches long for cooking, stirring, and loosening, and a nice set of either teakwood, ivory, or bamboo chopsticks for dining graciously; and

#3. A Silver Thimble to ease the time set aside for making clothing, curtains, and exquisite stitchery. (We were unable to find a thimble crafted in silver until four years after our wedding day. Only then did my mother consider us legally wed.)

Every household should have at least three (3) special containers:

#1. A bowl of fresh fruit, cleaned and ready for eating, to please the husband, the man of the house. A person should have at least three kinds of fruit each day.

#2. A jar or container filled daily with cookies or other goodies, to delight the children and their friends; and

#3. The most important of all, a vase or urn for flowers, to enhance aesthetics and embellish the environment.

Of course, remember the three assignments a person must do each day to justify being born a human being (not an animal, a duck, a pig, a mongoose, or whatever):

#1. Each day touch someone's life favorably;

#2. Learn something new each day; and

#3. Very important: Do something just for YOURSELF each day.

On the first day of each Chinese New Year, each bedroom is put in order, and each young person appears in new clothes and serves tea flavored with sugared sweetmeats, especially ginger, to parents and each other. Then, one by one, from oldest to youngest, each comes forward and kneels on one knee before each parent, both palms on the other knee and bowed head resting on hands. Each child recites the traditional blessing:

#1. Remember your ancestors;

#2. Honor your parents; and

#3. Always respect your teachers because they prepare you for a better life.

Money placed in red envelopes is given to each offspring, to be spent on something sweet and/or luxurious.

My mother thought that the third commandment should be repeated every day, not just once a year.

The Power of Three (3) continues:

When worshipping at home or at a Chinese temple, if stick incense is used, always three sticks are lit together and placed in the urn. When bowing before a shrine or at a memorial service, the palms of both hands are placed together and moved three times as the head bows three times.

When a helper of Buddha goes forward to sustain the masses, a member of the military walks on his right to protect him, and a scholar is at his left to help him make erudite decisions, a triumvirate of three majestic disciples serving the populace.

In preparing meals for the family, I had to memorize a phrase that would remind me of the basic three ingredients necessary in food planning. In Chinese, simply said, it was: "Hahm Ngee, Choy, Fahn," translated literally as "Salt Fish, Vegetables, Rice." The words "salt fish" meant a protein of some sort, "choy" a green vegetable, and "fahn," some sort of staple like rice, potatoes, noodles, or taro (a carbohydrate). Each category may be increased, but the basic ingredients for a balanced meal was there.

I also had to memorize categories of food and important condiments, herbs, seasoning for each, and how long to cook each. Seafood was lumped into three groups: Fish, Shellfish, and "Armored" Sea Animals. Fish was done when the eyes emerged popped. Shellfish (shrimps, prawns) were done when their backs curved round. Armored Fish (crabs, lobsters, etc.) were done when their shells turned red.

For each dish, at least three seasonings were used. More may be added, but the basic three came first. For spinach: garlic sauteed in oil, then a dash of soy sauce. For swamp cabbage: always ginger, oil, and a touch of raw brown sugar to bring out the taste. For Chinese eggplant: garlic in oil, hoi-sin sauce, and chili paste, to name a few.

Often the combinations of some seasonings have great medicinal value. A black fungus, often referred to as Wood Ears, with Chinese vinegar and dark soy sauce, is helpful in keeping blood pressure in check, besides being delicious when cooked with chicken. Sometimes a pinch of the raw brown sugar is all that is needed to enhance the taste of the food.

I was enthralled by the number THREE (3). I asked Mama, "Does that mean that a man can have only three concubines?" When she ignored me, I realized that I should not make light flippant remarks on so touchy a subject.

She did emphasize the importance of happiness in deciding a career choice. A person should feel free to make changes while seeking a vocation that is enjoyable and profitable, up to three times. By that time, the final, happy selection should be found.

I have shared some very personal thoughts with you, and leave you with these three special parts of me: my love, my thoughts, my goals, are of you, always.

Fall 2007

Chinese Funerals:
A Lost Tradition

Ah Po, my mother's mother, departed this planet at age seventy-two. At her funeral, the first of two days, her descendants gathered at a large funeral hall on each side of her body beautifully arranged in a casket, male descendants on one side, females on the other, seated on floor mats and large cushions.

As each visitor arrived, Ah Po's sons and daughters, taking turns, would tell of some aspect of the life of the deceased, in a high sing-song voice, such as…

"…She was eighteen years old when she came to Honolulu with her new husband…"

"…She was well-versed in culinary arts, beautiful stitchery, and knew the medicinal value and use of herbs…"

"...Tragically, at age forty-one, eight months pregnant with her eighth child, she was widowed..."

"...Maintained the family values she had developed with her husband: that one-third of everything earned must be set aside for family enrichment activities, such as music, drama and dance exposure, higher education for her SONS, and community outreach activities to help sustain other people's lives..."

All this and more, repeated and sung by both sides, (in Chinese, of course) male and female, as each guest arrived and walked around the casket draped in the center of the hall.

At one point, suddenly Mama sang out in a foreign language. People stopped in their tracks. All of the family members stopped wailing, and Mama, as she heard herself, looked up apologetically, slightly amused, and continued her sing-song sentence in Chinese. She had begun her greeting sentence with two foreign words she had just learned. She sang out:

"SOMETIMES SHE..." then stopped when she heard herself, and chuckled to
herself. Later she explained that she had been trying to learn this foreign language (English) and those two words just slipped out, but the occasion brought a semblance of humor to an otherwise serious moment.

"Sometimes she...would go for a walk by herself up some hills and look over the beauty of nature and give thanks for the opportunity of bringing up a family and instilling values of appreciation for the gift of life, not bemoaning her present status as a widow bearing this burden alone..."

Then, from the male side of the room, came the voice of her #3 son:

"...When I wanted to leave school and get a full-time job to help with the family finances, she absolutely would not allow it. Continued higher schooling has long-range values for a higher quality of life, she insisted. Stay in school, get a part-time job, and enjoy what you can as you grow..."

Mama, her #2 daughter, sang out, "…She heard of a shirt factory in downtown Honolulu looking for someone to sew buttonholes on shirts. She quickly sent me and Big Brother to apply for the concession. Because her feet had been bound since childhood, she had difficulty walking distances. We got the job. Every day we brought home a dozen shirts and then Big Sister and I helped her sew the buttonholes. Each shirt needed seven buttonholes (five down the front, one on each cuff). A dozen shirts meant eighty-four neatly hand-stitched buttonholes, for which she received fifteen cents. She quickly removed one-third, or five cents, placing it in a special container, saving it for family enrichment and community outreach activities, plus higher education for her SONS, and used the remaining two-thirds for household expenses and family needs."

"…She saw a need for experienced midwives, and was much sought-after when people heard of her skill at teaching new mothers-to-be a comfortable way of giving birth. She took a bed sheet, rolled it tightly into a long rope, tied one end to the rear of the bed, handed the other end to the laboring mother-to-be, who then pulled on the 'rope,' raising up to almost a sitting position…and OUT came the baby!!!"

"…included in her mid-wifery services were two concoctions she prepared to be eaten by the new mother: pig's knuckles brewed in vinegar, red wine, and special herbal spices; and chicken in fresh ginger splashed in whiskey. One for uterus contraction, the other for milk production."

Then came the singing voice of fourth Auntie (whom we lovingly called 'Baby Auntie'): "From her earnings she invested in stocks. To each of her sons she gave a hundred shares of City Mill stocks. Each of her daughters received five shares…"

The high-pitched sing-song wailing continued till midnight, when the lights were dimmed, but kept on for the occasional visitor who could only come after midnight because of swing-shift work hours. At seven we were roused. After washing up, we put on fresh white garments (the Chinese color of mourning), and ate a light breakfast of "Jook," a rice gruel flavored with Chinese sausage and spinach. After donning the capes and hoods made of a coarse off-white fabric, Fourth Brother whispered,

"...similar in shape and style to those worn by the Ku Klux Klan of the southern United States."

The family of Ah Po gathered outside the mortuary for the procession through the main street of Honolulu Chinatown. First in line were the sons of the deceased, then the daughters, then the grandsons. After that, the male spouses, female spouses, and then the granddaughters. I was at the end. There were several younger grandchildren, too little for the procession.

I remember feeling scared and so alone. Mama, Papa and my brothers were way up in front. As I, a lowly girl-child, stood at the end of the formation, looking bewildered and afraid, a pleasant-appearing lady, a family friend, came forward, took my hand, and said, "I will walk with you."

We walked the several blocks to Maunakea Street, the center of Honolulu Chinatown, where two bands were waiting for us, plus many friends of our family.

The lead band, consisting of drums and gongs, snapped to formation, and the parade began. Two mortuary attendants wheeled a large portrait of my grandmother, leading the procession behind the first band. At the end, behind me, marched the second band, with cymbals, strings, and a very high-pitched flute-like wind instrument, with sounds that Second Brother said could "wake the dead." Then followed others: close friends of the family, business associates, and "calabash" cousins.

Following the lead band, we paraded several blocks on Maunakea Street, turned left for several blocks, then left again toward the mortuary, where limousines were waiting to take us to the Manoa Chinese Cemetery in Manoa Heights. After interment, and offerings of food for the departed, three circular 8-hour incense rings were lit. It was now our turn to relax and share in the food for the occasion.

In response to comments made by some of the guests that an elaborate funeral observed in this fashion is usually just for men, it was announced that this day was special because this woman, widowed at age forty-one, eight months pregnant with her eighth child, had brought up her children, maintaining long-term family values, to become outstanding members of the community, was deserving of such a community remembrance.

FAST FORWARD almost three decades.

In 1960, on the occasion of my father's departure from this world at age eighty-one, the first day, with relatives and very close friends, was spent in preparation for the second day, open to the public.

The Manoa Chinese Cemetery had filled to capacity so a new plot of land was developed for future use by the Chinese community. It was off Nuuanu Avenue on the way to the Pali. Certain plots were reserved by families.

On the first day, relatives helped to prepare for the public's arrival the next day. A coin of silver needed to be wrapped in red paper, to be given to each arrival, and a package with a coin of lesser value to each person as he or she leaves. There is no way of knowing ahead of time how many packages of "red paper money" would be needed, so two hundred packets were prepared. As it developed, over a thousand people appeared, since my father and brothers were well-known. You can imagine the next day as relatives hurriedly gathered coins and wrapped them in red paper for the guests.

Mama, now a widow at age seventy-two, supposedly no longer with income, would need provisions to prepare for her new life after the hundred days of mourning, during which time only white (the color of mourning) is worn. As is the custom, relatives and close friends brought swatches of colorful dress fabrics, in three-yard-lengths, for the widow to make into "glad rags" to signify the end of formal mourning. Red ribbons that are woven into the hair at that time are donated by the mortuary.

As each length of fabric is brought in, the mortuary scribe writes in Chinese on a large square of gold paper, with a full-sized brush pen dipped in black ink, the name of the donor. Then an assistant affixes it to the ceiling to hang vertically. Since I did not think my husband's parents in California knew of this custom, I personally purchased a swatch of material and indicated them as the donors. The scribe reacted in puzzlement.

"How do you write WILKINSON in Chinese?" he asked. He finally decided on three words that had the sound of those syllables: Wai-Gun-Sun (not a recognized Chinese surname). That caused some puzzlement to some guests who were trying to determine the source of that particular swatch of fabric.

Talented close friends created, out of bamboo and temple-blessed rice paper, a yard-high three-story house, with butler and maid, plus a limousine and liveried chauffeur, for Papa to take with him. Mama commented, "He will be better taken care of in the next world."

Meanwhile my brothers and I were each busily folding (a thousand each) gold and silver paper money to be sent to the next world through fire the next day.

Traditionally, in ancient Hindu and Buddhist tradition, the send-off of a noted man is cremation on the banks of a river, hopefully the Ganges River, which is not practical in Honolulu. The body is taken to a river, a clump of wet mud placed on the navel, and the body placed on a pallet on stilts. After the fire (under the body) consumes the body, the navel (the source of life) remains un-burned under the clump of mud, and is sent back into the rushing river to continue its source of life.

In Papa's case, he was dressed in his best clothes in an open casket, with a large pearl sewn on a headband to light his way, and a piece of jade placed on his tongue to ensure he will always eat well and have good things to say. Each person performed an act of symbolic cremation. On a table by the open casket is a container of rice paper. A strip is picked up and lit by a burning wick in oil. Then, while still burning, the participant touches the body with it gently and puts the burning strip into a metal container next to the body, where it continues to burn until the paper is consumed. Each guest, all ages and genders, is afforded this privilege.

There were other performances. A group of sixteen professional civic-minded men, lined up in four rows of four each, recited in rhyming quatrains, with accompanying foot-stamping and handclaps, positive virtues of Papa's community outreach generosities.

After the temple activities, guests were invited to continue the celebration of Papa's life at Fourth Brother's home, where a caterer served a feast to all attending. So that each guest would eat well to a happy, serene, and comfortable old age as did my father, each guest received a celadon-glazed rice bowl, with the black teak chopsticks they had been using, filled with rice and five items of food: fish, pork, chicken, tofu, and vegetables, to be consumed later at home. When available, this ceramic pottery with the neutral celadon glaze is used, developed by the Chinese and borrowed and named by the French. The caterer has to prepare twice as much food as the number of people attending.

Sixteen years later, at age eighty-eight, my mother's spirit left this world. Having lived this long productively, assisting in the education of her sons AND DAUGHTER, she was afforded a funeral almost equal to that of a man.

In the decade prior to her passing, I was able to make frequent trips to visit her. Of course, I had no way of knowing how much time was left for me to enjoy her. She was most touched each time our whole family visited her, and expressed joy in seeing them as they grew.

She had prepared the clothing she wanted to wear on her trip to the spirit world, but could not find a pair of shoes comfortable for her to walk in. On one of my trips, she noticed my soft-soled Chinese slippers and found them most comfortable when she tried them on. I told her I would get a pair for her from San Francisco Chinatown so that her "afterlife" would be comfortable.

After the ceremony, this time we adjourned to a restaurant for the farewell feast. There had been two big funerals prior to my mother's, which exhausted the Island's supply of celadon-glazed rice bowls to be given on the occasion of noted senior's funerals. So we had to settle for some very attractive and more expensive rice bowls to be filled with rice and goodies to be enjoyed by participants at my mother's funeral.

In recent years one by one my cousins and brothers have reached the time of departure from this world. Whether it is that statehood has reached Hawaii, or there is no one left who remembers the old customs, or fewer people know of the ancient customs, or that English is the language spoken by the younger generation (not Chinese), the ceremony now lasts part of a day. The viewing is at 9:30 in the morning, with two or three speakers voicing remembrances of the deceased, and musicians playing Hawaiian or current "popular" music, and the guests lining up for the feast, buffet style, in the adjacent room.

Even with those cousins or my brothers who were in their late eighties, or nineties, or the recent one of my oldest brother, who was a hundred and one and a half, no special food was presented and taken home to symbolically honor the age of the decedent.

I have been asked to eulogize some of the persons we are honoring, usually to recall stories of early accomplishments. Of the thirty-one first cousins who were a part of my "growing up" memories, born between the years 1905 and 1937 (I was in the lower fourth), there are only eight of us left today. At the rate departures are occurring, there may be no one left to come to my funeral (or talk about MY accomplishments, or lack of them)!!!

27 July 2011.

About the Author

Born in Hawaii in 1922, May-Blossom Chang Wilkinson grew up in rural Wahiawa on Oahu, working in the family's Chinese restaurant, and interpreting for her Cantonese-speaking parents from the age of six. The youngest of five with four older brothers, Blossom attended the army school at Schofield Barracks, eagerly reading every book in the library before starting on a second round. She skipped two grades, from second to fourth, in one year. At age thirteen, she created her first paid job when she trekked twenty-two miles by bus to Honolulu to inform the Honolulu Star Bulletin that they needed a Wahiawa correspondent. They took her on, and she wrote a weekly article for the newspaper, highlighting local events.

After surviving the 1941 Japanese attack on Pearl Harbor, she attended the College of the Pacific in Stockton, California on scholarship. When she began her teaching career in 1949, she was the first Chinese teacher—and first teacher of color—in the Berkeley School District. Though the district was impressed that she spoke English so well and without an accent, they were concerned about how she would perform, so, for the first two weeks, they stationed two rows of university students in the back of her class to observe and document everything she said and did. She went on to teach first and second grade in four California school districts, including Redding, where she hosted an educational TV show, and San Mateo, where she spent the bulk of her thirty-eight years in the classroom.

In 1950 Blossom was invited to participate in a youth work camp in Germany, sponsored by the World Council of Churches, designed to bring young people together from all over the world to rebuild a youth hostel. In 1990 Blossom was part of a delegation to Russia, sponsored by the League of Women Voters, to advise women on how to be more assertive in politics.

As a teacher, Blossom's signature work was on the mathematics of Chinese paper folding; she conducted numerous workshops on paper folding as a tool for teaching math in primary grades. Over the years, she led many tours of San Francisco's Chinatown for elementary students as well as adults, highlighting the history of Chinese slave girls who escaped with the help of Donaldina Cameron. In 2011, Blossom was honored by the League of Women Voters of California.

The mother of four, Blossom has seven grandchildren and one great grandchild. She lives with her husband Bob in San Mateo, California.

Printed in Great Britain
by Amazon